EXCUSE PROOF LEADERSHIP:

A Get-It-Done System for Building a High-Performing Team

I0040309

EXCUSE PROOF LEADERSHIP:

A Get-It-Done System for Building a High-Performing Team

Tracie L. James

LaMorne Enterprises, LLC
2017

First Printing: 2017

DISCLAIMER

The purpose of this book is to educate and entertain. The author and publisher shall have neither liability nor responsibility for anyone with respect to any loss or damage caused, directly or indirectly, by the information contained in this book.

We don't believe in get-rich-quick programs. Your success is predicated upon your work ethic, delivering extraordinary value, and serving others with excellence.

We cannot and do not make results guarantees or give professional or legal advice.

ISBN 978-0-9990290-0-8

LaMorne Enterprises, LLC

P.O. Box 3288, Jackson, MS 39207

www.tracieljames.com

Just for buying this book, I want to give you a FREE gift. For a more in-depth online training on how to be Excuse Proof, visit TracieLJames.com/gift.

Dedication

This book is dedicated to my sons, Terrance & Mikal. You're my inspiration and the reason I work so hard each day. Love you both so much!! I want you both to see from my example that you can accomplish anything when you don't let excuses get in the way.

Table of Contents

ACKNOWLEDGMENTS

I would like to take a moment to acknowledge the people who have been with me on this journey to my purpose.

I would like to thank my family without whose support and encouragement this book would never have been completed. Thank you for ALWAYS being by my side. A special thanks to my late grandparents for instilling a love of knowledge in me.

A special thank you to my business coach and mentor Jonathan Sprinkles for pushing and challenging me every step of the way. You've been an inspiration and have become one of my dearest friends. Thank you for showing me my worth when I doubted myself. You're truly the personification of walking in purpose!!

To three very dear friends who were catalysts for this journey to my purpose:

To Steve, you saw what God saw in me and never gave up on getting me to see it. Thank you for always being the voice of encouragement and honesty. I miss you dearly, but I know you're in a better place. You're no longer in pain. You will always be my angel. RIP

To Shelby, you lit a fire under me that could not be put out. You pushed me to want more for my life and my business. Thank you for saying what needed to be said, even though I didn't want to hear it.

To Felix, you've inspired me, motivated me and advised me. Thank you for praying for me and for pushing me into greatness. You truly helped me to Wake My Successful Self Up!!

To my dance coaches, Dr. Josephine Kelly, Larry Thurman, and Bridget Archer, you taught me to never make excuses and to take responsibility for my growth and development as a dancer and ultimately as a person. You truly gave me the foundation I needed to be successful in life and business. Thank you for never letting me give up even when I struggled.

Thank you to my editors who provided me with all the needed feedback to make this book the best it could be.

To my dear line sister, Toni, you opened your home to me and helped make my transition to Houston smooth. Your words of encouragement helped me keep moving forward. Thank you for personifying the sisterhood of Alpha Kappa Alpha Sorority, Inc. Love you!!

To my girls – Monique, Wendy, Noel, Sallee, Kim M., Kim B., Kim R., Kim G., Tara, Regina, LaShawnda, Geilia, Jenean and Sherie, thank you all for being there to encourage, support, and pray with and for me all these years. I truly appreciate your sisterhood. Love you all so much!!

To Christine, you've been my support team since I began this journey. Thank you for sharing your talents with me. You make me look better than I am. You're awesome!!

I am so grateful to have each of you in my life and on this journey with me. Thank you for being a part of my journey to become the woman I am today.

PREFACE

My childhood dream was to become a dancer and choreographer like Debbie Allen. I saw this as my way out of Mississippi and my opportunity to live an exciting life. I wanted to perform and travel all over the world. It just seemed so much more glamorous than the way the people in Mississippi lived. I spent a huge portion of my childhood following her life and wanting to pattern my life after hers. I read everything written about her and watched every TV show or movie she did.

In junior high, I took my first real steps toward accomplishing this dream. I made the dance team and so began my life in dance. I had been dancing before, but just at home in front of the mirror. Performing with the dance team made it all seem real for the first time. I continued my training into high school and was so looking forward to graduation. My plan was to attend Howard University in Washington, DC. This was the college Debbie attended. I was excited to walk in her footsteps at Howard.

My college plans took a major hit when I found out I was pregnant. My heart still wanted to follow in Debbie's footsteps, but I had to attend college locally so I could have help raising my son. Initially, the idea of attending Jackson State University was a tough pill to swallow. I had to put my dream to the side so I could be a mom and a student.

I started college just a couple of months after having my son. Navigating freshman year and being a teen mom was no easy task. I was successful, but not without hard work, many sleepless nights, and a lot of tears. I cherish every moment of my time at JSU. I answered the challenge of juggling motherhood and college student. I was on a full academic scholarship so I had to maintain no less than a 3.0 GPA. That's no easy task without a child, but with a child it required some sacrifices to make sure everything was handled. I didn't handle it perfectly, but it turned out perfect.

When I walked across that stage in May 1994, I smiled as I remembered the night I almost gave up. My son had been sick and I had a big paper due the next day. I had barely slept and still had to type my paper. I had finally gotten my son to sleep on my lap. I was afraid to lie him down so I just kept him there while I typed. It was almost midnight and the paper was due at 9am. I got frustrated because I had typed the same page like three times. Remember this was in 1990 before word processors or home computers were widely available. I needed to do footnotes and it just wasn't working for me that night. I began to cry and was about to get up from the table and go to bed. I looked down at my son lying in my lap so peaceful. I knew he was depending on me so I wiped the tears from my face and went back to work. I didn't make it to bed until almost 4am, but I got the paper done. My son was my motivation to never give up, even though it was hard. I could have used being a mom as an excuse for not finishing college, but I made a different choice. I decided it was my motivation.

This motivation enabled me to continue to be successful throughout my career. I wanted to set the example that no matter what happens in life you must find a way to accomplish your goals. My drive to find solutions is rooted in my dance training. My coaches never allowed excuses. They pushed us to work hard and learn the technique. There were no shortcuts to being a great dancer. You had to put in the work and never give up.

When I look back, I see how I carried this lesson with me in all I did. My dance experience is the foundation of my leadership skills and all the success I found professionally and personally. Having a "no excuses allowed" mindset helped me through being a teen mom, finishing college and ultimately success in Corporate America. If you struggled with a dance step, you kept working on it until you mastered it. I applied the same mindset as a manager... always look for the solution.

I worked hard and found success in every position I held in my over 20 year career in Corporate America, nonprofit organizations and government. I was consistently promoted in retail and then moved on to work in various outside sales positions in the consumer products industry. I faced the challenges head on because I wanted to be an example to my son that no matter what happens, you make it happen. No excuses allowed.

My career has been a mix of success, layoffs and new challenges around every corner. Often, I didn't realize what I was facing until later. I was so ambitious and determined to be Vice President of a major corporation that I just did whatever I had to do to stand out. I take pride in the fact that I consistently hit and exceeded sales goals throughout my career. I was often called upon to assist with training of new staff. I faced the challenge of entering new industries and quickly adapted to find success.

I am proud of being named Top Account Manager, winning sales incentive trips yearly and being consistently promoted. If only they knew what all I had overcome to be standing there. I had to juggle the responsibilities of being a single mom with the expectations of being a corporate executive on the rise. The long hours of working and all the travel meant I was away from my son a lot. I had to make arrangements for his care in my absence. I often indulged his requests to make up for being gone so much. Many nights, I cried myself to sleep in hotel rooms in some other city because I really wanted to be home at his football games.

Despite all of these successes throughout my career, I was still searching for the right place for me. There was a feeling deep inside of me that wanted to do so much more. Whenever I shared that with people, they didn't understand. Let me paint the picture for you. I was making 6 figures, driving a company car, with an expense account and traveled all over the country. I had been breaking through barriers throughout my career because I never let the excuses stop me. I didn't let being the youngest or the only black or only woman stop me. It motivated me. But here I was just steps away from opportunities in senior leadership in a major international corporation, but I was unhappy, and in many ways depressed because I felt like a failure as a mother.

I started to look for new opportunities, but none of the jobs appealed to me. A glimmer of an idea came as I flew home on a red eye flight from Las Vegas to make it to my church to help with the youth event that Saturday morning. Deep in my heart, I wanted to do work that made a difference not just made money. Now, I had to figure out how to make that happen.

A few months later, I decided to step away from my corporate position and go to work at my church. Over the next few years, I successfully developed summer and afterschool programs for churches and non-profit organizations in the area that focused on academics and the arts. I felt amazing every day until I looked at my bank balance. It was rewarding in every way except financially. I took a MAJOR pay cut – like 75% less.

This impulsive leap of faith was not working out like I had thought it would. I had to make some adjustments so that I could support myself and still live a life of purpose. I spent several years working multiple jobs, often 7 days a week. I felt it was worth it because I was determined to live my life on my terms. My entrepreneurial journey has taken many turns from consulting with churches and nonprofit organizations to dance instruction.

This journey took a shift in 2015. Two key events sent me on a journey to discover my true purpose in life. I attended an event to support my friend Shelby, who is a life coach. I enjoyed her event and afterwards we had a conversation that really set me off. She asked about my business and I told her about what I was working on. She paused and then told me that I didn't have a business, but a bunch of projects. This hit me in my gut hard. I was honestly mad, but I couldn't be upset with her because in my heart I knew it was true. Her comments haunted me for months.

A few months later while I was with my friend Steve, I received a call that I got often from someone wanting to "pick my brain" about an idea they were considering. After I got off the call, he asked me what I charged for my services. I sat there unable to speak because I had not charged for my consulting services in years, especially not friends.

After this conversation, I recalled something my Grandmother Eva told me when I was around 11 years old. She said I would be an educator like her. She had been a dedicated teacher for over 30 years. I didn't want to hear anything about teaching. Remember I wanted to be Debbie Allen. My grandmother wanted me to embrace my journey, but at the time I was young and wanted to be someone else.

All of their comments made me realize that I had been sitting on my purpose this entire time because I had not monetized it. Strategy came so easy to me that I forgot that at one time I charged for my skill set. This conversation gave birth to the seed my grandmother planted many years ago. Finally in my 40s, I was ready to embrace my purpose and who I am naturally. I am an educator, a developer and an encourager. My work now is centered on educating, developing and encouraging leaders to their full potential.

Now, you have the opportunity to learn more about how I've been able to succeed despite all the obstacles I've faced. You will learn how to be an Excuse Proof Leader.

INTRODUCTION

"Ninety-nine percent of the failures come from people who have the habit of making excuses."
George Washington Carver

I magine this...

An office is full of busy, hard working people who work effectively together. Their leader sets the example and works daily to motivate, inspire and develop the team. Everyone effectively communicates and is doing exactly what is expected of them each day. Goals are achieved consistently and the team is never complacent. Everyone is motivated to do better than they did the day before. The team is empowered and feels appreciated for their talents and skills. No one ever makes an excuse about missing a goal or deadline. They find solutions for the obstacles that are blocking their success. Nothing stops this team from hitting the mark.

Have you ever experienced this? If not, then this is the book for you.

We live in a world that does not operate like this well-oiled machine described above. There is hope because there are organizations that come really close to this perfection. This type of excellence in team leadership occurs when a leader is focused on developing an excuse proof culture. No excuses given and none accepted.

Let's look at this a little closer.

To be an Excuse Proof Leader, you must first define what an "excuse" really is. Research over the years has defined excuses as denial and justification; some view excuses as a type of lie, deception, or a half-truth; while for others only certain excuses are lies. An unknown author defined it as - "Excuses are tools of the incompetent which create monuments of nothingness. Those who specialize in them are seldom good in anything." An excuse has absolutely no value.

My definition is "Excuses are an attempt to escape the consequences of actions taken or lack of action taken; a desire to justify your current situation or to explain away failure to meet expectations." Excuses do not enable you to take responsibility for your actions.

People are motivated to make excuses for impression management (a desire to impress someone significant or a gap between real and ideal or imagined self) or they feel the situation calls for it (teacher/parent acts as the judge of good and bad excuses; could improve the outcome; or self-image is put in jeopardy by threat).

Excuses are considered self-handicapping behavior by psychologists. Self-handicapping behavior is described as behavior that hurts our own performance and motivation. As a result, excuses affect how you think about the goals you're setting. Excuses affect how you approach the plan you've made to accomplish your goals. If you do not change your mindset and the mindset of your team, you will get caught in the excuses and never perform to your highest potential. It doesn't matter if the excuse is based in fear, doubt, being uncomfortable or worry about what other people will say, you still have to move on past it.

Excuses keep us from realizing our full potential. Giving an excuse does not enable us to learn from our mistakes and make changes for the future. Failure is an opportunity to learn, but if all you do is excuse your way out of every failure you never learn. You just keep blaming someone else or a situation for your lack of success. No real success can occur in this space.

We often accept excuses because we don't want to confront the person giving the excuse. The avoidance of conflict is real. When you call someone on their excuses, you must be willing to ask questions and not let them off the hook. In addition, if you hold someone else accountable for their excuses, then you have to hold yourself accountable. Stepping up to the plate to take full responsibility for your mistakes and missteps is not easy, but necessary.

It's easier to accept the excuses than to do the work to face your fears and doubts. The journey to success is not easy, but you can make it there. You just have to do it regardless. Put in the work even when you're afraid or doubt whether you and your team can accomplish the goals you've set. Don't give up. You've come this far. You shouldn't give up now. Take the leap. Be courageous and go after it with everything you have. Inspire your team. Motivate them to get past the excuses that are ringing in their heads and keep putting in the work on the plan you've laid in front of them. Be the example and let them follow you. Remember to focus on leading instead of managing your team.

It's simple to say remove the excuses, but it is not easy. You must become accountable what the things we do regardless of whether we're right or wrong. Personal responsibility is real and needed if you want your team to be successful. Creating a culture of personal responsibility begins with you as the leader. Set the example. Be transparent. You must be able to admit when you fall short and make changes to make it right. Your team will follow your example. They will accept you holding them accountable because you hold yourself accountable.

Productivity suffers when your team is not operating at their optimal level. It costs you more to get less done when your team is not motivated. When you have a team that constantly focuses on: "what if we don't succeed" "what if we fail" "what if we don't get the contract" "what if the product doesn't sell", the goals will be lost in the midst of the negativity.

Employees lose credibility when they use excuses more than once. Justifications, like slim resources or tight deadlines, cause people to no longer trust their ability to do their work effectively. Employees that do not trust that their co-workers are dependable will not operate at the best level. They will either be resentful of having to pick up the slack or give up because they feel overwhelmed by their inability to complete tasks consistently.

You must understand that the person that is stuck in the cycle of giving excuses does not experience consistent success. They spend much of their time blaming others for their current situation. They are stuck and unhappy with their life and their job. They tend to be pessimistic about change.

They never offer new ideas and have no interest in growth opportunities. Challenges are avoided at all cost. They often set themselves up for failure by giving excuses all along the process.

There are many reasons for why your team underperforms. First, your team may have a level of insecurity. If your team does not feel they can answer the challenge, they will make excuses for why they didn't hit the mark. Second, no one is comfortable admitting that they did not understand what they were asked to do and often refuse to ask questions then struggle to figure it out. Unfortunately, they often do not figure it out and are unable to effectively complete the project or task as requested. Lastly, a lack of commitment and determination keeps people from completing their work on time and in excellence. When a person does not have a desire to do their best work, they will underperform and pass the blame.

You should be concerned about the effects of excuses because it impacts your ability to successfully lead your team. Your team will not achieve its goals if you're constantly dealing with a barrage of excuses from your team about missed deadlines, missed goals and low quality work. If you're determined to be a successful leader, then you must address this issue head on. Don't ignore it. It will destroy everything you're trying to build.

Your company can suffer financially when excuses go unchecked. Nearly 29% of company time is unproductive – the equivalent of 33.5 days per worker per year. The estimated cost of this lack of productivity is nearly $600 billion per year in the US. Think about what that means to your company's bottom line. What are you losing each day when your team is not productive?

Excuses impact your profitability and productivity. Your reputation and business relationships can be impacted by your willingness to give and accept excuses. You will not be seen in a good light by other leaders when you're constantly dealing in excuses. They will not trust that you and your team will do the work effectively. In addition, you will lose your best employees because they cannot function in an excuse laden environment. The ones that stay will be the ones that are constantly underperforming. It's not a good situation from any angle.

Basically when you give excuses, you are not taking ownership of your results. You are not taking personal responsibility for what happens at the end of the day. You are quick to accept the accolades for success, but when failure occurs, you are quick to shift the blame. A true leader doesn't just take credit for what went right, but responsibility for what went wrong. When you remove the excuses, you can really get to work on building a team that is productive and motivated.

I wrote this book out of frustration with excuse laden organizations. I'm a solutions minded person and I have a strong desire to working in excellence. I cannot function when I'm surrounded by excuses. I have to battle my own excuses in my head. The last thing I want to do is deal with it from other people in the workplace. I decided it was past time to confront this issue that continues to be ignored and swept under the rug. It's imperative that leaders address this issue now and stop treating the symptoms. Let's pull up the root cause of underperformance and failure – EXCUSES.

When I trained as a dancer, excuses were not allowed by my coaches. They pushed me to the next level as a dancer by teaching me that no growth occurs when you are constantly making excuses for why you haven't mastered the technique. They created a culture where excuses didn't survive. We learned from them how to be successful not only in dance competition, but in life. I applied these principles in the classroom and in corporate America throughout my career.

Excuse Proof Leadership is a get-it-done system for building a high-performing team. This approach to leadership removes all the excuses and negativity that surrounds us each day. You focus on the goal and outline a pathway to that goal, despite all of the expected and unexpected things that can occur.

As the leader, you are like the dance choreographer. You're responsible for making sure everyone is in proper alignment, using the right footwork, in the correction formation, highlighting their skills throughout the choreography, and making constant progressions and variations as needed.

As the choreographer, you start by working with your team to build your relationship and gain valuable information about your team. This information will help you identify the right actions for consistent success. In addition, you will be able to more effectively set goals and share them with your team.

Next, you will learn about your team's strengths and will be able to more effectively delegate tasks so you can be focused on the tasks that deserve your full attention. Lastly, you will build an excuse proof culture that will help your team avoid complacency. It's a simple, yet effective approach to leading your team.

When I say "Excuse Proof Leadership", I want to you embrace the mindset necessary to drown out the excuses that are running through your head and to develop a plan for how you will deal with your team's excuses. As a leader, you are often attempting to do something that's never been done before, as a result you can't see a path that's already been laid out. You must blaze new trails for your team. Your team will follow and push past the excuses when you set the example and debunk the excuses that are in their heads.

Throughout my career, I've held leadership positions in non-profit organizations, corporations, politics and ministry. As a result, I've learned the importance of leading instead of managing. You will be your most effective when you embrace leading your people instead of just managing. You manage resources or things, not people. You can fully control resources or things, not people. People have the option to follow or not. When you remember this, you will find a different way of being a manager... or rather a leader.

8

Let's make a comparison of the two. If you take the time to compare the mindset of a "manager" vs. the mindset of a "leader", you will see a very clear delineation.

Managers	Leaders
➢ Focuses on maintaining stability	✓ Focuses on creating change
➢ Creates rules	✓ Breaks the rules
➢ Plans all the details	✓ Sets the direction
➢ Executes the culture	✓ Shapes the culture
➢ Avoids conflict at all costs	✓ Uses conflict to make improvements
➢ Seeks out the tried & true methods	✓ Seeks out new ways and opportunities
➢ Takes credit	✓ Gives credit
➢ Makes decisions & tells the team	✓ Facilitates decisions through team involvement
➢ Tells the team the vision	✓ Inspires team to follow the vision
➢ Transactional style	✓ Transformational style

You cannot manage past the excuses. You must lead your team past the excuses. Don't leave them there. Just inspire them to keep their eye on the ultimate goal. Being a transformational leader is like being the captain of a sports team. You are on the field with your team executing while leading them to victory. They know you and you know them. They trust you and you trust them. As a result, no excuses matter.

Responsibility is the antidote for excuses. You must commit to shifting the culture from one of blaming to one of personal responsibility and accountability. As an Excuse Proof Leader, you will not accept anything less. Your team will work harder and be more engaged when they take full responsibility not only for their role on the team, but also for the results achieved. Each person will have a great sense of accomplishment with each goal reached. This will be the motivation for them to keep striving. Keep leading them to each new level.

I learned so much about leadership as a dancer, dance team captain and dance instructor/coach. The dancer that has to fight and work hard for every move can be pushed and stretched to greatness. While the dancer with natural ability and no work ethic will only go as far as their natural abilities can take them. They get frustrated easily when things don't come easy for them. They look for short cuts and are constantly blaming others for why they can't do it. As a former dance coach, I will take the dancer who takes personal responsibility for their growth over the one with natural ability that expects everything to come easy. Excuses do not make world class dancers like Misty Copeland. She would not be where she is today, if she had leaned totally on her natural ability. She put in the work and didn't let anything stop her from accomplishing her goals. I call her the Excuse Proof Ballerina!!

The 5 DOs to Excuse Proof Leadership

The 5 DOs diagram showing "Excuse Proof Leadership" in the center with five surrounding circles: Do It With Them, Do It Right, Do The D.E.W., Do You... Delegate the Rest, and Do NOT Settle.

- Do It With Them – Lead from within your team
- Do It Right – Right Actions + Dedication + Consistency = Success
- Do the D.E.W. – Detail Everything in Writing
- Do You... Delegate the Rest – Effectively utilize the strengths of every member of your team
- Do NOT Settle – Avoid complacency

Within this book, you will learn how to implement each of the "5 Dos" to excuse proof your team. As we take this journey to shift your leadership style, I want you to takes notes so you will not forget those key thoughts later. This book is your opportunity to assess your current leadership style and see what aspects you're missing that will improve your ability to build the high performing team you need to reach your goals consistently. You will find that some techniques in this system will come naturally to you, but others you will need to be intentional with implementing them. You will begin to see changes when you truly commit to this system. So much of it comes from committing to the mindset shift of not allowing anything or anyone to come between you and your success, even if that one thing is you.

Take action now to lead your team to its full potential and stop making excuses for why you aren't as successful as you could be. My system will help you and your team to not be slowed down by the excuses. You will see measureable improvement in your results if you effectively operate consistently without excuses. This is not a one and done system. You must remain focused on the process and continue to work on it throughout your career. My desire is to help you be a better leader that is successful regardless. Be Excuse Proof!!

Assess Your Team

What excuses do you currently hear from your team?

_____

_____

_____

_____

What is your current way of addressing these excuses?

_____

_____

_____

_____

Based on what you've read so far, do you feel you need to make some changes?

_____

_____

_____

_____

DO IT WITH THEM

Excuse Proof Leadership

Chapter 1

"Do It With Them"

"Leaders get more done working with their team, instead of above them." Tracie L. James

Effective leadership is important to the success of your team or organization as a whole. What does effective leadership look like? Effective leaders are great team players. You must understand the importance of leading from within the team. As the leader, you can get more done working with your team; instead of above them. While working within the team, your team learns that no work is beneath you and that you won't ask them to do anything you are not willing to do yourself. Without a doubt, leading by example has been proven to be more effective than leading by telling. When you take the time and "Do It With Them", your team will be in proper alignment to be more effective and more productive.

Proper body alignment allows the dancer to move freely and lessens the risk of injury. Poor body alignment puts excess strain on muscles and joints, while proper alignment helps to strengthen the dancer's muscles. Learning proper alignment, or body carriage, is often the first step in learning to dance. Within your organization when your team is not properly aligned to the vision and mission, your organization will suffer the consequences. So often we see these issues, but we do not address them. We just make excuses and keep moving on in the hopes it will just go away, but it doesn't. Excuses create a contagion or ripple effect throughout the organization that affects productivity and profitability. Having your team in line with you and the vision will net the bet results.

Please understand that I'm not advocating that you do your team's work, but they must know and respect that you are willing to work as hard as they are to achieve the goals. Your team can teach you about what they know, especially when the task is outside of your comfort zone. You develop a stronger bond with your team when you work with them, in comparison to other team leaders, who make demands and wait for the desired actions to take place.

When you make the transition into management or business ownership, you may be unprepared for such a demanding leadership role. Be proactive and determine the type of manager or leader you are. Some leaders believe they need to push their team. Others feel they need to pull them along. A few decide to take the lead and bring their team along with them. There are some key flaws with the first two options. When you push, or pull your team, you do not know what their reaction will be. The reaction may or may not result in good performance or resistance. The morale within the team environment may change for the worse.

Being a leader that is not afraid of rolling up your sleeves and getting your hands dirty, demonstrates a willingness to understand and listen to your team. Show them and they will listen. Do not be afraid to jump in the trench with them. If all you want to do is bark orders, then you'll never make that leap into true leadership. True leadership is leading without ego.

I have been blessed to work with some great leaders. For example, my sales manager when I was a retail merchandiser did an amazing job of "Do It With Them". He took time each quarter to work with me. He would assist me with visiting different markets and working in the stores with me. He would not take over the visit, but allowed me to maintain and build my relationships with my accounts. He would assist with product checks and educating the owner on the hair products we supplied to this retailer. He effectively supported my efforts consistently. He was better able to advise me because he had taken the time to visit my markets so he had information upon which to base his advice.

You can see examples of this type of leadership and how effective it is in many of the success stories you read in newspapers and magazines every day. Studies have been conducted to determine why these leaders are so successful. I have read the articles and listened to the leadership profiles on the news about amazing CEOs, who revolutionize an industry. As I read, I noticed that there are a few characteristics in common, but one key element caught my attention. Each organization possessed employees who were fiercely loyal to the organization. The loyalty can be attributed to the trust that the employees had in each leader, which was built by the way they've worked within their organizations.

Two corporate giants that stand out for me are Bob Townsend, former CEO of Avis and Herb Kelleher, co-founder, Chairman Emeritus and former CEO of Southwest Airlines.

Under their leadership, these companies experienced growth and market success. Many attributed their success to their understanding of working with people and willingness to lead without ego. There are countless stories of them doing work on the lines with their people and never attributing the company's success to what they've done, but more to the collective effort of great people.

For example, Bob Townsend became CEO when Avis was struggling and had never made a profit. From 1962-65, the "We Try Harder" promise advertising campaign was birth and it helped to transformed the company in just three years. His unique leadership style involved him spending time working the Avis rental counter. He considered this to be so important that he required that every employee, regardless of position, to go through agent training. Working directly with your team, like Townsend, provides first-hand knowledge that a report or survey does not capture. In the process, he got to know his employees and they got to know him. The results showed in their profits and also in employee loyalty.

Another example is Herb Kelleher former CEO at Southwest Airlines. He is legendary for the atypical, fun-loving environment he created in the airline industry. He set the example by working the ticket counters, handling baggage and serving drinks during flights once a quarter. His leadership style transformed this commuter airline into the major airline it is today. Under Kelleher's leadership the airline has grown from three planes in 1971 to a fleet of more than 680 planes.

Many employees have stated that Kelleher's leadership inspired their desire to work at Southwest Airlines. Kelleher inspired people to perform at their best and to contribute to the success of Southwest Airlines. He operated Southwest like a "family". Everyone is valuable to the success of the organization. Each employee takes ownership of making sure each and every customer has a great experience while flying Southwest.

Personally, I learned early in my career that if you're willing to start the work with them, they will finish it. I started my career in retail management at the young age of 21. I had been in the management training program for 6 months. Now that all the final presentations were completed, we were receiving our assignments. The company had stores in Mississippi, Alabama, Louisiana and Florida. I was terrified because I had no idea where I would be placed and I had a young son to consider. If I turned down the assignment, I would be forced to go find another job so I was terrified. I knew someone always ended up staying in Jackson and I so wanted that to be me.

Well, I did not get my wish. My assignment was in Birmingham, AL. I was moving to a new city the week before the Thanksgiving. I had no idea about this new city, the store or any of the people working there. I had never lived away from home and I was so afraid of leaving, but I had no choice because I had no other job options. Plus, I really enjoyed working in retail and it was what I had worked so hard for the last six months.

I had just over a week to prepare to leave for Birmingham to report to work. In that time, I had to adjust to the idea of being without my son for the first time in 4 years. I was not sure if I was doing the right thing leaving him behind, but the company did not give me any time to set up daycare for him or any help at all so I had to go initially without him. The plan was to bring him over later. The stress of leaving my son only magnified the stress of moving to a new city and the unknown of the new store. Regardless, I had to make this work because my son was depending on me for support.

I had completed management training, but was totally clueless about what to do my first day in the store. When I arrived, I was greeted by my new store manager and assistant manager. They gave me a quick overview of my new department and the existing staff. I was going to be managing a staff of 12 sales associates. Over half of my staff had been working in that store for over 10 years. The rest of my staff had been there at least a year and this was their first job in retail. I immediately realized I needed to figure out how to be successful with a team, whose experience was so varied. Honestly, I doubted my ability to lead this staff. I knew I did not want to be the manager who barked orders and made demands. I never responded well to those types of managers.

My first week in the store, I spent most of it getting to know my staff through casual conversations on the sales floor. I felt that casual conversations were my best course of action.

Since I started with the company as an associate, I understood the sales floor, like the back of my hand. I would spend at least 30 minutes working with each sales associate. During our talks, we worked the sales floor. We completed such tasks as putting out merchandise, straightening tables and racks, and assisting customers. I wanted to learn about my staff's personal experiences, their family, and their interests outside the store. I wanted to build a foundational relationship with my new team. I knew from my past experience that when you build a good relationship your team will do anything to support you in achieving the goals of the department. It was good for morale and the overall experience of working in the store.

Ultimately, I gained my staff's respect and trust because they saw my willingness to work alongside them. I wanted my staff to know that I did not consider any job on my sales floor beneath me. Through my leadership style of "Do It With Them", they responded by working hard. I set an example and my staff followed. Working together helped us achieve the department goals. I built a cohesive team, which resulted in my promotion to the second highest sales store in the company after a year of working with my staff. In addition, one of my fulltime staff applied for my position and led the team upon my departure. This staff member became another leader, who achieved great success with the company.

In the beginning, when I took this approach with my team, I built rapport with my staff and treated them fairly. Since I enjoy talking to people, I was very comfortable talking with my staff while we worked together. My staff was able to see my work ethic and value my impact as a team leader. Even now, as I shop I straighten merchandise on tables and racks. Hard work is just in my blood.

Unfortunately, leaders often fail because of their understanding or perception of a leader. Their perceptions and understanding surrounds the belief that a leader is someone who tells others what to do. These leaders lack an understanding of the process involved in being a good leader. When you are a leader in title only, you just tell people what to do and walk away. In my opinion, a true leader works alongside their team to ensure they have an understanding of what needs to be done and how it should be accomplished. This clarity helps them be successful and ultimately feel empowered to do the job they were hired to do. It also gives them a positive image of the person that is leading them. The team is aware of what is necessary for them to do their jobs. The team gains respect for the leader instead of developing fear or resentment. You don't want people that only work when you're watching or standing over them. You want people to be bought in on the mission and you can accomplish so much by taking a little time to build that working relationship.

As you are building your relationship with your team, you can more effectively define the goals and develop a path to the goals. Planning together enables you as the leader to manage the expectations of your team. Since you understand the issues of managing the project or department, you can help your team navigate them better since you're working with them. You must answer their questions effectively and in a timely manner. Being a great talker can move them to action, but being a great listener can keep them there. When they know you're really listening to them, they will respond by fully supporting the vision you have laid out. This type of leadership will enable you to develop authentic relationships.

This team environment can grow further when you recognize them for the work they do and show true appreciation. Encourage your team to try new things and make it safe for them to fail so that you can promote innovation. Be sure to provide motivation, inspiration and encouragement so that you can build trust with them. The success of your team depends upon how strong a relationship you build with your team.

Effective communication is one of the keys to a successful team. When leaders work with their team, they are better able to establish open lines of communication – formally and informally. Alex Pentland at MIT's Human Dynamics Laboratory took on the task of identifying what makes a great team.

The study found the following:

- Communicate frequently.
- Talk and listen in equal measure, equally among members.
- Engage in frequent informal communication.
- Explore for ideas and information outside the group.

The key connector in each of these areas is communication. So it is imperative that you work with your team to build the lines of communication with everyone. The benefits will be increased interaction, conflict resolution, clear understanding of individual responsibilities, and informal training.

When your team is stuck in a cycle of making excuses, your team will not be able to function at its optimal performance level. They must take responsibility for what is and isn't happening each day. When you work with your team, you can more effectively identify what and who are blocking the team from success. Once you have this information, you can make adjustments and better train your team for success.

When you work with your team, you can address two of the main dysfunctions of a team, as identified by Patrick Lencioni, namely the Absence of Trust and Fear of Conflict.

People's natural reaction is to trust when they feel safe. As a leader, you must make your team feel safe. Your team will trust you more as they get to know you have their best interests at heart. Not just as an employee, but as a whole person. True engagement from your team can occur when you engage the entire person. At times, a person is disengaged because something negative is happening in their life personally. They may love what they do at work, but they're weighted down by the pressures of life – issues in their relationships, health issues, financial issues, etc. As a leader you must empathize and let this person know you care. As their personal life gets back in balance, you will see more engagement in their work life.

We always accomplish more working with people than we can on our own. Collaboration is an amazing element that will enable you to do more in less time.

To Build a Good Team

- Open Minded
- Diverse Group of People
- Build trust
- Open Communication
- Positive Environment
- Clarity of vision and goals
- Accountability

When you work with your team, you can impact employee engagement. Research has shown that 68% of employees are not engaged. Of those that are engaged, 32.5% are fully engaged and are hard at work consistently; 51% totally disengaged and are just along for the ride; and 17.5% are just trying to sink the boat. If you're interacting with your team, you will be able to identify everyone on your team and where they fit in this context. Then you will be able to manage them accordingly.

In this part of the system, you're the player/coach. You're leading but you're working with them on the field as well. You must be able to see the big picture, but also get into the details at times to ensure your team understands the plays completely.

While working with your team, you need to learn what motivates each person. Motivation is not a one size fits all concept. Each person has both positive motivations (productive) and negative motivations (counterproductive).

The goal is to maximize the motivations that are productive while minimizing those that are counterproductive. For example, you can have a high performer that is great at their job, but has toxic behaviors when their ideas are not accepted by the group that can suck the life out of your team with their overly aggressive, temper tantrums, etc. They are motivated to be the best, but bring the team down with their negative behavior. You must find ways to minimize the effect they have on the entire team.

ACTION STEPS

1. **Do schedule time to work with your team on a regular basis, especially when new employees are hired.**

Determine how you will work with your team – on the sales floor, one-on-one meetings, sales calls. Working with your team creates an environment of trust and loyalty. Work with your team on a regular basis regardless. Establish a routine that demonstrates the importance of working with your team. If you don't put it on your calendar, you know it will get lost in all the other tasks on your To Do list.

2. **Do demonstrate the work you expect.**

While working with your team, be sure to demonstrate the type of work you expect from them. Leading by example is more effective than leading by telling.

3. **Do clearly explain what needs to be accomplished.**

Based on the size of your organization, establish clear lines of communication. Everyone is not comfortable just walking up to the boss and offering their ideas. Create an environment which encourages team work and collaboration.

4. Do create an excuse proof culture.

Be sure to let every employee know that the expectation is for them to find solutions for any issues they present. Excuses must be solved. Excuses will only be addressed with a positive mindset.

Application of "Do It With Them"

I have a client who took over as the general manager of business. She entered the business and found so much resistance and lack of communication. Everyone was so possessive of their jobs and didn't want anyone else to know what they were doing. They all had excuses for why they didn't see the need for meetings and for sharing information. They just wanted everyone to only know about their role. I recommended that she implement these action steps to get to the root of the issue.

She was met with some resistance at first, but slowly she was able to build the trust. She found that everyone was afraid of being replaced. They wanted to be valuable by being the only person that could do what they did in the business. This format is great for the insecure employee, but detrimental to the business as a whole. Customers depended upon service from the entire business not just one individual area.

Ultimately, she was able to improve the communication between departments and help everyone understand that the goal was to better serve their customers not take over anyone's job. Taking the time to build the trust, she now knows what's happening in the business at all levels and can effectively lead her team to success. Collaboration is now the foundation of this business.

REMEMBER THE BENEFITS

- Excuses will block your team's potential from being fully realized.
- Builds trust and inspires them to follow you.
- Learn more about your team and their abilities.
- Develop an environment that encourages collaboration.

Assess Your Team

How do you currently work with your team?

_____

_____

_____

_____

What is your current process for assessing your team's strengths and weaknesses?

_____

_____

_____

_____

Based on what you've read so far, what changes do you feel you need to make?

_____

_____

_____

_____

DO IT RIGHT

Excuse Proof Leadership

Chapter 2

"Do IT Right"

"Establishing the right actions will turn a mountain into a hill." Tracie L. James

Whan you determine the right actions that will get you to success, you can excuse proof your team. Clarity is the enemy to excuses. Excuses should be used as an opportunity to find solutions. Ask questions to get to the right actions that will get you past that excuse. The excuses are standing between you and your team and the success you are working so hard to accomplish. You must remove them so you can focus on the real work that needs to be done.

It's not just hard work that will lead to success. You must be working hard in the right direction to achieve the goals you've set for your team. If your goal is to the left and your team is pushing hard to the right, you will miss your goal no matter how hard they work.

The Old Success Formula

Hard Work + Dedication + Consistency

Your team must make the pivot from "Hard Work" to "Right Action" to more effectively work toward the goals that have been set for the team.

Hard Work

↓

Right Action

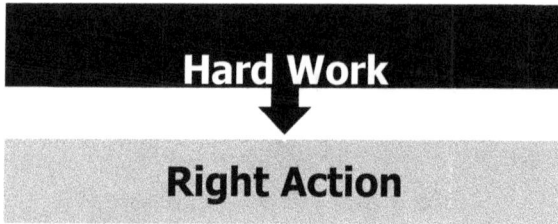

Once your team pivots from hard work to right actions, your success formula will work properly. Combining the right actions with dedication and consistency will enable your team to find success over and over again.

The New Success Formula

Right Action + Dedication + Consistency

I see the right actions like the right footwork for a dancer. Dance technique requires that the body be in proper alignment and the correct placement of the feet occur. In ballet, the right footwork begins at the ballet barre. Here is where the foundational principles are taught. These principles instill the importance of discipline, commitment and consistency. Once a dancer finishes their work at the barre, they then move to center floor work where they build upon the technique they have already learned. You can't move to the center floor until you've completed your barre work. Structure and discipline are the keys in developing a great dancer and a great leader. As a leader, once you master the basic leadership principles, then you can use them to build upon later.

You lead your team to the right actions and make sure they are clear on what the right actions are to get them to the success you seek. So how do you determine what the right action is for your team?

When you make the decision to excuse proof your team, you must learn what has helped you be successful so your team will know what actions to take consistently. What actions have you utilized that positively impacted your results? What steps are needed to get to this desired result again? Taking time to assess what worked and what didn't work will enable you to establish actions that your team can use to consistently achieve the success you desire.

Every team needs a clear plan of action to operate effectively. This goes beyond an organizational chart. It's about how you do business each day and can "Do IT Right" repeatedly. The establishment of the "Do It Right" actions reduces inconsistencies within their work and provides everyone on a team the security of knowing everyone's place in this and how we each contribute to the success of the whole.

When you repeat the right actions, get feedback, adjust as needed, then you will reach your goals more consistently. Document what you're doing consistently to reach your goals. Your team will be able to assist you with determining what actions are working and which ones are not. Use your data to help you zero in on what it takes for your team to be successful.

4 key elements to consistent success:

- **Right mind** – being positively motivated
- **Right heart** – being sold on the purpose & mission
- **Right skills & talents** – building your team with the talents and skills you need to accomplish your goals
- **Right focus in the right direction** – focused on the goals and the right actions are outlined in the plan to get there

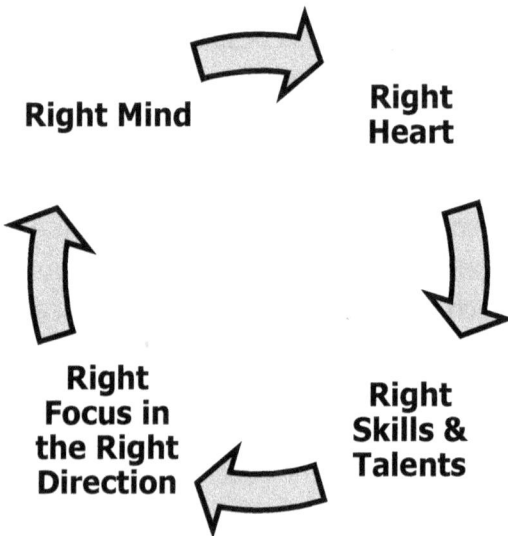

Right Mind   **Right Heart**

Right Focus in the Right Direction   **Right Skills & Talents**

Gaining clarity will improve your team's motivation. When they know what they need to do to be successful, they will be confident they can get the job done. Your team must be inspired to accomplish the goals of the team. Without their dedication and commitment, you will not be able to implement the right actions to get to your goals.

You cannot take your eye off the wheel. You must assess your team's progress consistently. Get their feedback and adjust the plan as needed. You don't adjust the goal. You just adjust the plan to get there. Being flexible is so important to being successful. If you are on the wrong path, then you must be willing to adjust to get on the right path.

Once you establish effective actions, your team will operate more efficiently. Your team will be empowered to work without a lot of supervision and will ultimately increase your team's collective ability to get more done in less time. Having these actions written down will enable you to more effectively train new employees. The ability to reduce the learning curve is critical for day to day business activities.

People struggle with consistency because of distractions, a lack of focus, lack of commitment and being undisciplined. You must find ways to counteract these issues on your team. You must help your team shift from a desire for quick results to a focus on long term results.

One critical area of focus for the "Do It Right" action is in the area of customer service. Customer service can make or break a company. In this age of social media, customer comments placed online can spread quickly and ruin a company's reputation in a matter of hours. Very successful companies have established customer service actions that are truly customer focused. Not just in word but also in deed. Let's take a moment to look at a few of the companies that continue to be successful and are considered to be the best in customer service too.

Amazon is considered to be the best online retailer when it comes to customer service. Many people will only shop online with Amazon because of it. If your order is lost in transit, you can call their customer service line and a new package will be shipped immediately. Very few questions asked and no blame is placed on the customer. They just correct the issue and deal with the lost package with the shipping company. Talk about great customer service. Their employees are empowered to take care of the customer. No calling for a supervisor to approve anything. The action enables the employee to deliver the best customer service possible immediately. This creates an environment for fierce customer loyalty.

Apple is another company that has fierce customer loyalty. If you have ever been in an Apple store, you experienced a conversation with staff that truly love and believe in the products they represent. They make sure you're getting the right product and you understand how to use it once you leave. Their tech service is so top notch that customers wait for appointments and rarely consider switching from Apple. The right training action for their staff ensures that their customers are taken care of no matter where you are in the world. That's a powerful "Do It Right" action.

I have another example of what happens when you use a "Do It Right" action. As a former dancer, I am impressed by professional dancers around the world. These dancers must be at the top of their game for years to build a successful professional career. As I mentioned earlier one of my favorites is Misty Copeland called "the unlikely ballerina" by

The New Yorker in 2015. Copeland has effectively taken not only the ballet world by storm, but mainstream media as well. Like business managers, dancers are trained and developed based on key foundational principles. When you commit fully to those foundational principles and use them to build upon for your success, you can express uncommon success. Misty not only used those foundational principles by practicing relentlessly each day to be the best each time she hits the stage. She also employs the same determination in building her legacy outside of dance. Her advertising campaign with Under Armor took the world by storm just before she was named the first African American principal ballerina at the American Ballet Theatre (ABT). This advertising campaign was different because it highlighted how different she was from traditional ballerinas and how she persevered at being herself and found her success.

Misty used what every dancer learns at the barre to overcome an injury that many thought would end her career just a few years before she accomplished her goal of dancing for ABT. Her determination to "Do It Right" day in and day out regardless of the naysayers enabled her to become the world class ballerina she is today. She knows what it takes to be successful consistently and puts in the work to make it happen. Now, a new generation of dancers can follow the "Do It Right" action she followed so that they have no excuses.

Personally, I learned the importance of "Do IT Right" when I started working as a merchandiser for Proline Hair Care Products early in my career. I replaced an individual, who left the company without prior notice and failed to leave any materials for my transition into the position. As a merchandiser for Proline Hair Care Products, I was responsible for retail accounts across the state, including national retailers, independent beauty supply stores, and distributors.

I held this position in 1996 when sales people did not have cell phones, a GPS or Google Maps. I mapped my territory by hand. Using a map of the state, I divided it up into 4 sections. Then, I planned my route for each area, ensuring that I could visit all the major cities within each section. During my first visits to these cities, I created my account list, which enabled me to determine what areas would require most of my time. After about a month, I had created a list of the entire state. Using this list, I was able to develop a clear action for effectively managing the entire state. This list included not only my route, but also critical information on each retail location. Each manager, whom I encountered, had a different expectation of merchandisers. I made note of these expectations for each account so that I would know each time I visited their store. The action helped me to be successful in my position. As I traveled to each section of the state, I did not miss any of the retail accounts I was assigned. In addition, I built relationships with each store manager because they saw me consistently and I respected their individual expectations. As a result, many of these managers partnered with me on promotional events to support the sale of our products in their stores.

I could have given up when I found out there was no documentation for the area, but I did not. It was a tough time traveling and not knowing where stores were located, but that time paid off. I decided to not allow the excuse of the hand I was being dealt stop me from succeeding. I stayed focused on my success goal and just created a new path to it, literally and figuratively.

When I have changed companies or industries, I remained successful for two main reasons. First, I identified the similarities and applied my knowledge of these similarities accordingly. Second, I tapped my skills as an effective communicator, listener, problem solver and negotiator. These skills enable me to operate with different people and still experience success. Everyone operates differently and you will have to adjust your action at times accordingly.

For example, I worked with a buyer at a small locally owned grocery store. When I first started in the position, he never wanted to meet with me. He refused to give me an appointment. I had to do some research and ask questions of people who had worked with him in the past. I adjusted my action of managing accounts to meet his expectations. He wanted to know in advance what we would discuss. He would only accept this information by fax, no email. If he considered the meeting necessary, his assistant would call to set up a meeting. Once I adjusted my action for account management, then he met with me. In the end, he was one of my best accounts and I loved to visit his stores.

Being a leader that chooses to excuse proof your team, you must take managing to a new level. You must focus on the things you can control. You create an effective action for what you can control. You make adjustments for the things you cannot control. The goal is always to maximize the potential of your team by helping them develop good habits, which will be the foundation for every action you create.

Remember you can build a dedicated, high performing team by doing the following things:

- Know what your team's expectations and needs are and be sure they are clear on your expectations
- Be accessible and social
- Build a relationship with your team
- Be transparent
- Don't micromanage
- Be respectful
- Don't use fear as a motivator
- Reward and praise regularly
- Train your team effectively and develop them for leadership
- Meeting with your team regularly
- Lead by example
- Create a culture of accountability
- Challenge your team to their potential
- Lead with integrity

ACTION STEPS

1. Do focus on what you can control.

Take the time to know what areas you can control and which ones you cannot. Focus on what you can control. There is no such thing as a "perfect" action; only one that is effectively implemented. Once you have implemented a new action, give your team time to see some results. Analyze the results and make any needed adjustments until it is working as it should.

2. Do make your action flexible and adaptable.

Since change is the one constant, leaders must manage that change effectively. See the change as an opportunity to do something different. Empower your team to make changes to a action, as needed.

3. Do make the difficult decisions.

Leaders must be willing to acknowledge issues and seek solutions to fix them so their team can succeed regardless. You must stay away from excuses and stick to the solution. Be a "fixer".

Application of "Do It Right"

I have worked with businesses to develop a more effective way to build relationships with their customers. I helped a restaurant build better relationships with their catering customers. Their catering business was doing well, but it could have been much better. They felt like they were constantly trying to get new customers and their repeat customer business were very small. After assessing their business, I realized that past the initial thank you for their order, they had no contact with their prior customers. They were waiting for them to call back to make another order.

The right action for them was to set up time to make calls and/or send emails to prior customers to see if they could cater another event and even offer a repeat customer discount. As they began to implement the right action, they began to see their catering business grow. They even needed to hire a part-time person to assist with the growth they experienced. When you find the right action and implement it consistently, then you will see better results in the long run.

REMEMBER THE BENEFITS

- Help your team get better results consistently.
- Empower your team to make decisions.
- Establish accountability within your team.
- Increases the level of commitment from each person on your team.

Assess Your Team

Do you currently have processes in place that your team uses on a regular basis? If so, are they written down?

_____

_____

_____

_____

Do you currently have any issues with inconsistent results? If so, what are you doing to address those issues?

_____

_____

_____

_____

Based on what you've read so far, what changes do you feel you need to make?

_____

_____

_____

_____

Excuse Proof Leadership

DO THE D.E.W.

Excuse Proof Leadership

Chapter 3

"Do the D.E.W."

"Great leaders know how to focus on the detail without losing sight of the full vision." Tracie L. James

When you establish goals with your team, you will map out a plan for getting to each goal. This plan will enable you to assess predictable "what ifs". These "what ifs" often lead to excuses when the goal isn't reached. Eliminate these excuses on the front end by asking questions and putting contingencies in place for them.

A choreographer begins with a vision in mind for each routine choreographed. There is a message or visual image in their minds. To communicate this to the dancers, the choreographer must take the time to clearly lay out their ideas. This will include writing them down in addition to communicating them verbally and physically. As a part of this planning process, the choreographer will use stage directions to let each dancer know where they need to be on stage throughout the routine – upstage, downstage, stage left, stage right or center stage. In addition, each dancer must know where the other dancers will be on the stage so they will not be any on stage collisions. Being in the right formation at all times is key to a beautiful performance.

As a leader, when you make the vision clear and outline a clear path to that vision, you're setting the stage for your team's success. The structure and organization are needed to keep everyone on the same page. The written document is there for reference as a reminder to everyone on the team.

Leaders miss out on opportunities for success because their vision was not clear or the vision was not effectively conveyed to their team. Your vision must be clearly defined. Lewis Carroll says, "Any road will get you there, if you don't know where you are going." Knowing you want to be successful is not enough to make your vision a reality. Great leaders are focused and driven. You can impact one of the five dysfunctions of a team identified by Patrick Lenocioni - inattention to results – when you detail everything in writing. Written goals give your team a clear focus to compare to the results. You must "Do The D.E.W." and clearly Define Everything in Writing.

Do the D.E.W. is an important step to make sure your team is headed in the right direction. You cannot effectively work together to achieve anything if everyone is not clearly focused on the same vision. Your vision must be clearly defined and effectively communicated. Once you clearly define your vision, you must break the vision into goals that will lead your team to the vision. These goals will be checkpoints along the path to the success you desire. The vision should align with the values of the company. Ensure that the goals of the organization correspond with its core values. If not, it will lead the company away from the original intention of the organization. When you define your vision and goals, clearly define each and share them with your team members.

There have been numerous articles written over the years about the importance of writing down our goals, but so many still just think about their goals. When you write down your goals and regularly focus on them, you're 42% more likely to achieve them based on a study conducted by Dr. Gail Matthews at Dominican University in California. Writing down your goals connects the right and left hemispheres of the brain by taking what you see in your imagination and writing it down to connect with the logical side. Creating that connection increases your ability to make the needed changes to accomplish your goals.

Writing down your goals and clearly defining them for your team reduces confusion. Your team can ask questions for further clarification and it helps everyone be on the same page. You cannot achieve a goal if your team is unsure of the path to the goal. When you "Do the D.E.W.", you outline the goals and the path to the goals you're setting for the team.

You hear so often about people creating vision boards for their goals each new year. It's become more and more popular as research has shown that people are accomplishing these goals because they are in front of each day. Having written goals will help your team do the same thing. Their goals are right in front of them each day.

Written goals will help your team take ownership of the goals that are set. Researchers at Cornell University found that the "endowment effect" occurs when a person takes ownership of something. Giving your team clear goals that they can own from beginning to end with increase their dedication, commitment and ultimate success.

Over the years, I have found the use of the S.M.A.R.T. method to be very effective for defining my goals and objectives with my teams.

S – Specific: State exactly what you want to accomplish - who, what, where and why.

M – Measureable: Quantify the goal so that progress can be monitored.

A – Agreed Upon: Get consensus from your team; including accountability.

R – Relevant: Goals should be consistent with other goals. Be sure no conflicts exist.

T – Time-based: Set a deadline for completion of the goal. It must have an end date.

When you assess each goal with these parameters, you can be sure to not only have a goal, but also a pathway to that goal you want to accomplish. Your team can be more successful as a result. As the leader, you've given them what they need to complete their assignment without excuses.

Throughout my sales career, I either managed sales associates or industry brokers. Regardless of my position, clearly detailing the goals for the month, quarter and year was very important. Having a discussion about the goals was not as important as writing them down. Once the goals were written down, I established an agreement between all involved parties who were stakeholders.

The goal setting process with my sales staff was very different from the process with industry brokers. My sales associates were motivated to maintain their employment and receive bonus money for hitting and exceeding their goals. Brokers were independent business owners and they had the same expectations as the corporations. They needed to maintain a level of profitability. They wanted the company to be successful in placement of products because ultimately it impacted their company's bottom line.

While working for Sara Lee HBC, I worked with brokers who assisted with the distribution of our skincare line to independent beauty suppliers across the United States. Most brokers covered a specific region, so I juggled each one separately. At first, I was overwhelmed. My new position came with more responsibility and more travel. I went from traveling only in my car to flying all over the country.

I learned my lesson quickly during the first quarter. I was pumped and ready to be successful. I was the youngest person in my position for any brand in the division so I knew I had to prove myself. The first quarter did not go well. I struggled to get a handle on my national retailers and the independents. I looked at my numbers and I was not happy with my performance.

I set up calls with each of my brokers to discuss what had gone wrong during my transition. What I found caught my attention. I know I had meetings with each of them during my first month and we discussed goals, but I realized that they weren't clear on what we discussed. This was my "aha" moment. I need to do a better job of clarifying by writing everything down.

Going forward, I would send them the goals for the quarter and follow up each week with updates on our progress. In addition, I would ask for suggestions and feedback on what was happening in their area. I took trips to work their areas with them so I could get a better understanding of their accounts. By the end of the next quarter, I was seeing improvements. The last two quarters of the year got me back on track to not only meet the year end goal, but to exceed it.

In addition, I gained the support of my brokers because I invested the time in them and their businesses. I had to do more than throw a number at them. I had to help them plan and assess consistently. Since my brand was one of many brands they represented, I had to provide them with quality information consistently to remain top of mind. We became a team because they knew I wanted them to meet their personal goals as well. We worked together to make sure we all succeeded.

Doing the D.E.W. is effective personally and professionally. You begin to live your life when you have clearly defined vision and goals. Otherwise, life is living you. Help yourself and your team by putting in the work on the front end so that your success will be on the back end.

ACTION STEPS

1. Do clearly define the vision and mission for your team.

Great leaders do not shy away from asking the question of "why". Why do you do what you do? Why does your business exist? Once you can clearly answer your why, then you can effectively communicate it to your team. To lead your team, you must first inspire them with your "why". The vision and the mission are the foundation for your goals.

2. Do define the goals that will enable your team to accomplish the vision and mission.

Setting clear, relevant and quantifiable goals are necessary for the success of your team. As the leader, you must get your team to agree to work toward the common goals. Your team must work effectively together along the path to your goals. Taking the time to assess your goals according to the S.M.A.R.T. goals process will increase your team's ability to be successful.

3. Do ensure everyone understands the path to the goals.

Once you have set your team's goals and established the deadlines, your team is ready to move forward. Ensure they are clear on what their responsibility in the process. This is the foundation of your culture of accountability. The plan will be easier for your team to follow if it is clear. Maintain an open line of communication with your team so you will remain informed on what's happening.

4. Do manage any risks to your team's success.

Assess your team's progress throughout the journey. You must be mindful of any potential risks to their success. You must adjust the plan as needed for these risks. When you involve your team in the risk assessment process, they will be even more committed to the process because you've included in the process.

Application of "Do The D.E.W."

One of my former clients owns a small clothing boutique and she really wanted to grow her business, but she was struggled with her newly hired employees. After meeting with her and her staff, I identified that she had some issues with focus and clarity on her team. They wanted to do a good job, but were unsure of how to do it and what was most important. I worked with her to clarify what her top three goals were for her team in the next six months. Then, we prepared some materials for her team that would help maintain focus.

She presented the three goals to the team and allowed them to ask questions about the plan to accomplish them. She included them in the process of identifying what worked with their customers. After the meeting, she put up posters with the goals in the break room area. She even posted sheets at the counter near the register to remind them to upsell and to ask for email addresses. After a couple of months, she began to see results with repeat customers and an increase in dollars per sale. With everyone on the same page and the goals clearly posted, they were finally on the same page and headed toward success.

REMEMBER THE BENEFITS

- Everyone has a clear understanding of the vision and goals.
- S.M.A.R.T. goals will be established.
- Accountability will be solidified in writing.
- Goals will remain top of mind for everyone on the team.

Assess Your Team

What is your current goal setting process? Is your team involved in the process?

_____

_____

_____

_____

How do you currently communicate goals and plans to your team?

_____

_____

_____

_____

Based on what you've read so far, what changes do you feel you need to make?

_____

_____

_____

_____

DO YOU...
DELEGATE THE REST

Chapter 4

"Do You... Delegate the Rest"

"A great leader effectively delegates the work needed to accomplish the goal." Tracie L. James

When roles are clearly defined, everyone knows what's expected of them and everyone else on the team. When you delegate effectively, you will manage with a more balanced approach with your team. Be the choreographer that effectively implements "Do You... Delegate the Rest".

Once a choreographer has communicated the vision for the routine, they will begin to teach the choreography. The goal will be to utilize the dancers and showcase their best skills. It's an expectation that professional dancers be well rounded, but everyone will have those techniques that they've mastered better than anyone else. A great choreographer will use these talents and spotlight them. As a leader, this is what you must do with your team. Delegate and develop their skills and talents so they shine brightly.

Effective delegation is just as simple as teaching a line dance. You will show them the moves, and then you will teach it to them, do it with them, make corrections, watch them and let them go on their own. No choreographer wants to have to dance with their group on stage for them to perform at their best. You want to watch them shine on their own.

It's very important to take the time to learn what your team's strengths are. At times, we may overlook an employee that is quiet and just does what's asked. This person often has many more talents that have yet to be tapped. When you "Do It With Them", you will capture the information you need to help you better delegate and empower your team.

Learn what your team's individual long term professional goals are. Based on this knowledge, you can begin to give opportunities for your team to try new tasks so they can learn new skills sets. They will embrace the opportunity when they know it will help them accomplish their ultimate goal. It will also enable your team to be more successful because you can engage more of your team in the right roles.

Remember that you cannot do everything and be successful. It is imperative that you develop effective skills in delegation. The most effective and successful teams are the ones that utilize each team member's strength to accomplish the goals. When you know your strengths and the ones of your team members, then you can eliminate the excuses. This is why successful leaders surround themselves with people who are great in those areas they are weak. Be smart enough to "Do You... Delegate the Rest".

Delegation is not always an easy task to accomplish and requires you to be confident in yourself and your abilities, while trusting others and their abilities. You can succeed much faster and sustain your success by building a team rather than by working alone. Consider delegation to be an opportunity to develop your team. A commitment to develop your team will enable you to maintain the success for the long term. You are developing the next generation of leaders when you give them responsibility for new tasks.

The unfortunate thing is that most leaders do not know how to effectively delegate, which limits their ability to be successful. Amy Gallo, Harvard Business Review, discusses why delegation is a critical skill. "Delegation benefits managers, direct reports, and organizations. Yet it remains one of the most underutilized and underdeveloped management capabilities."

Why do leaders underutilize this key aspect of their leadership skill set? A study conducted in 2007 by Institute for Corporate Productivity (i4cp) found that 46% of companies have a "somewhat high" or "high" level of concern about the delegation skills of their employees. Despite the high level of concern, less than 30 % of these companies provided any type of training in time management or delegations skills. It takes training and practice to improve your delegation skills. If companies truly want to increase the use of delegation, they must train their leaders to do it more effectively.

In addition, a study conducted by Hubbard & Garicano on delegation at law firms found that partners that effectively delegated earned 20% more than their counterparts that did not. In addition, top lawyers earned at least 50% more because they learned to leverage delegation to increase their productivity. You can be blocking your ability to increase productivity and your income by not delegating. This is an important skill to master since managers are consistently expected to do more with less. If you don't delegate, you will not be able to effectively keep up with the workload.

This is especially true for entrepreneurs. A 2014 Gallup Study found that entrepreneurs who effectively delegated saw their company's three year growth rates rise 112 percentage points ahead of their counterparts that did not. Mastering delegation can be the difference between owning your job or owning a business.

You may find yourself unable to let go of tasks and end up micromanaging your team. There are three reasons this is not good for your success or for your team's development. First, leading your team in this manner will destroy any trust because your team will feel you do not trust them to do their jobs. Second, you will be unable to develop your team to go to the next level in their professional careers. Leaders make other leaders. Lastly, your team will not feel empowered to do their jobs and they will wait for you and your team will not be productive.

You must get past the excuses that stop you from delegating effectively. So much of why you're not delegating is grounded in a place of fear. You must let go of the fear and fully embrace your team's skills and talents so they can help you be successful.

Are you feeling any of these fears when you consider delegation?

Fear of Delegation					
Failure	Quality of Work	Losing Control	Losing Time	Bothering Them	Them Doing Better than You

- **Fear of Failure** (What if they can't do it?)
- **Fear of the Quality of Work** (I can do it better. I'm a perfectionist.)
- **Fear of Losing Control** (I can't give away my authority.)
- **Fear of Losing Time** (It takes too long to explain it.)
- **Fear of Bothering Them** (I don't want to impose on them.)
- **Fear of Them Doing Better than You Could** (I'm insecure.)

Your team has untapped potential that delegation can use to take your team to another level. Develop your team by delegating to them. Free up your time for the tasks that no one else on your team can do. This is an effective way to manage your time and increase your productivity.

While I was a retail manager, I learned firsthand the importance of delegation. When you have a sales floor to run from 10am – 9pm every day, you realize you must trust your team to do the work because there is no way you will be successful alone. Learning my team's strengths enabled me to trust them in those areas when I could not be there on the sales floor. As the manager, I was often in meetings and dealing with reports. My team has to deal with customers and maintain the entire sales floor.

For example, I trained several of my full time sales associates to act in my place when I was not on the floor. These were seasonal professionals that could handle most customer issues that arose each day. They would shadow me on the floor when I had to deal with customer issues. Leading them by example and allowing them to ask questions afterwards so they could understand why I made my decisions. As a result, my department consistently had the fewest customer complaints. My staff hit their sales goals because we were a customer focused department.

Throughout my career I've had to learn to delegate. Without a doubt working for a non-profit organization pushes you to delegate. I was an event manager and responsible for a major fundraising event. I was the only staff partner on the event so I depended heavily on volunteers. This can be a challenging process since they are not employees. You truly have to depend on why they have chosen to support the organization to get them fully engaged in doing the work. I recruited volunteers for specific needs on my committee and found that this was more effective than just sending out a general request for volunteers. People responded because they liked the organization and was willing to do the specific work I needed done.

For example, I needed five people to assist me with managing the volunteers the day of the walk. This team assisted with recruiting these volunteers, getting them assigned to specific areas and overseeing them the day of the walk. This component working well was key to the success of the event. Each year, we needed approximately 350 volunteers to assist at the walk from the starting area, along the route and at the finish line. Without their help, I could not have managed this event effectively. Each person had a specific area they were responsible for and a group of volunteers to oversee. In a sense, they helped me be everywhere at the same time. Delegation works and helps you succeed regardless. They could handle issues within their area and seldom needed me because I made sure they had all the information they needed to manage.

When you delegate, you develop and equip your team for success. There are two main benefits to you as a leader. It will enable you to focus on other tasks that require your expertise and you are positioning the next generation of leaders. You can create a cycle of training and equipping by encouraging them to train the next person in line. If your people know you value them and want to help them become better, then they will work even harder for the company. Commit to developing your people through delegation.

Do not be afraid to admit that you have weaknesses. Surround yourself with people, whose strengths balance your weaknesses. Allowing other people to demonstrate their expertise has benefited me professionally. Throughout my career, my team has helped me accomplish my goals without feeling overwhelmed. Embracing delegation is a key element in my success regardless of where I've worked and what obstacles I've faced. Embrace your strengths and invite others to embrace theirs.

ACTION STEPS

1. Do assess the strengths and weaknesses of you and your team.

A personal analysis of your strengths and weaknesses enables you to identify the gaps in your ability to be successful. As a leader, you must seek to improve your abilities and often you can do this by surrounding yourself with people who fill those gaps. You can focus on further developing your strengths.

As a leader, you should be interested in developing your team. When you know the strengths and weaknesses that exist on your team, you can begin each person's development journey. This analysis will help you hire the right people because you will know what gaps exist on your team in respect to skill set.

2. Do assess your current time constraints.

Look at what tasks you need to do that you do not have time to do because you're busy handling routine tasks. Shift yourself from being "busy" to being "productive".

3. Do identify which tasks you can delegate to your team.

Set clear expectations for the tasks you need to delegate. You match the task to the team member that is best qualified to do the work or requires the least amount of training to take over the tasks. You will then be free to focus on the areas where you can effectively move your team further. Your team's collective effort and focus will lead to your team's success. Build your team and your business by valuing what everyone brings to the table.

4. Do set up a delegation process to use going forward.

You will find that once you delegate it will get easier. You and your team will be more confident and everyone will be more productive. As you identify other tasks that can be delegated, you now have a process that includes training, goals and management of the tasks.

Application of "Do You...Delegate the Rest"

While working with churches, I saw this issue of no delegation up close and personal. Many pastors who founded their churches are uncomfortable letting go of control in certain areas of their ministry. It amazed me that these awesome men and women of vision found it difficult to let go and empower others in the ministry to take the lead. This often led to them losing great leaders and destroying their personal health in the process.

I had one pastor who was so adamant that no one would step in his pulpit except him to preach. He did not like having guest ministers. He didn't want any other minister in the church to preach on Sundays. He began to lose great leaders because they were determined to be in a ministry that would use their gifts fully. He never took a vacation. His schedule affected his life and his health. His ministry was growing and he needed the help. It was there, but he was afraid to accept it.

I encouraged him to talk with me about why he didn't want anyone else to lead in the ministry. He was truly afraid of being betrayed. He had watched other pastors lose their ministries to people they empowered to help them lead. He was determined that this would not happen to him. I saw this is a crisis of faith as well as a very human trait of being possessive of what we create. He had to let go of his fears and trust that the ministry would be protected.

It took some pushing, but I was finally able to get him to agree to let a minister that had been with him over 5 years to preach one Sunday every other month. This would free him to rest and travel, if he desired. In addition, I encouraged him to meet with his ministers regularly and as he learned their talents to empower them to lead different ministries within the church. Over time, he began to relinquish some control. As he saw, his health improved and the ministry continued to grow. He felt more comfortable and built trust with his ministry team. The ministry as a whole was more productive in the community and was better able to serve the members.

REMEMBER THE BENEFITS

- Focus on your strengths and not feel overwhelmed.
- Develop the next leaders of your organization.
- Be more successful by using everyone's strengths.
- Build a culture of accountability by sharing the duties with your team.

Assess Your Team

How do you currently delegate to your team?

_____

_____

_____

_____

Are there tasks that you should delegate but haven't? If so, what's stopping you?

_____

_____

_____

Based on what you've read so far, what changes do you feel you need to make?

_____

_____

_____

_____

Excuse Proof Leadership

DO NOT SETTLE

Chapter 5

"Do NOT Settle"

"Leaders know that success is a journey not a destination" Tracie L. James

Complacency on your team often occurs after your team worked hard to achieve a major goal or came through a tough time. If your team answered a difficult challenge, you should be on the lookout for complacency to set in. Your team will be mentally and physically tired. You will need to provide encouragement and time for reflection on their accomplishment, but not so much that they get stuck there. Continue to push them to the next level.

Progressions in dance are movement done in succession across the floor. These movements are done moving in a forward motion. As a leader, you must keep your team moving in a forward motion and avoid complacency. Dancers must push the limits of their minds and bodies consistently to remain successful in their profession. A complacent dancer never improves their technique and will not be successful.

Leaders must do the same thing for their team to remain successful. You must help your team to progress through success, failure and the desire for perfection. You cannot allow your team to get stuck in either space of "comfort".

If you're unsure of whether your team has become complacent, then look for these signs:

Disengagement	Lack of Initiative	Lack of Innovative Ideas
Lack of Interest in their Personal Career Goals	Afraid of Taking on any New Risks	Taking Shortcuts
Lack of passion	Lack of vision	Lack of hope

If you're seeing any or all of these on your team, you do not need to hesitate any longer. You need to address this immediately. If left unchecked, the productivity of your team will suffer. You must find ways to re-ignite their passion by creating a sense of urgency around the next set of goals. Seek their input to spark their creativity to bring innovation back to the team.

An excuse laden organization is more likely to be complacent. When excuses are consistently accepted, then your team will continue to lack the passion, focus, and determination to accomplish the goals that have been set. You will not be able to gain consensus or buy in. You will not receive the best of what your team has to offer you when you just let their excuses ride without being challenged. Challenge brings about innovation and a desire for innovation can motivate your team to work.

When your team has a culture of constant movement toward being the best and never wanting to be second, they will not fall into complacency. Every team member needs to have a do not settle mindset. The team will regulate itself when the expectation is to keep innovating. Team members will help each other stay on the right path. As the leader, you set the example. You do not settle. You do not accept excuses. You challenge the excuses and seek solutions for getting past them consistently. Your team will follow your lead.

There are six major causes of complacency. Most importantly, there are also six solutions to address each cause.

Causes of Complacency

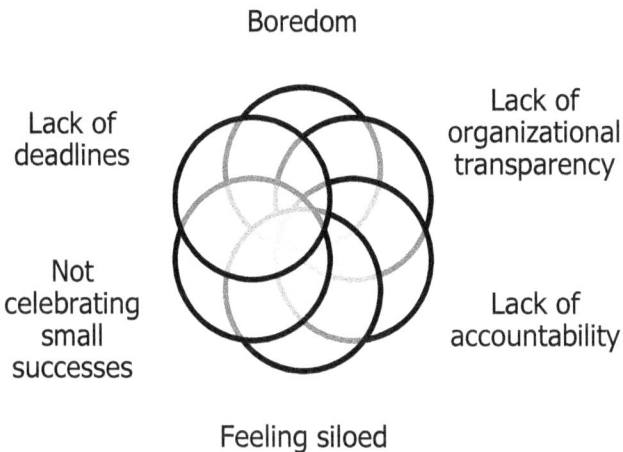

Boredom

Lack of deadlines

Lack of organizational transparency

Not celebrating small successes

Lack of accountability

Feeling siloed

Ways to Address the Causes of Complacency

Boredom – new projects and new opportunities keep teams energized

Lack of organizational transparency – in this day of layoff & companies shutting down, a level of transparency about how the company is really doing is important to build trust within your team.

Lack of accountability – each team member must be held accountable for the work they are expected to do consistently.

Feeling siloed – enable team members to work together on new projects to help each other to diversify the work they do; new perspective can spark innovation

Not celebrating small successes – don't just wait for the big goal to celebrate; make a practice of giving consistent pats on the back to your team

Lack of deadlines – be sure that all of your projects have clearly defined deadlines; when team members feel what their working on has no sense of urgency, it will be reflected in their work.

Your path to being a great leader will not look like anyone else's path because you will not be the same leader they are. So, stop comparing yourself to others. Glean the lessons from their experiences, but keep it moving. You must continue to lead no matter the situation or the level of the problem's complexity. Leaders with a no excuses mindset take what is thrown at them and build a strong foundation for success. This is what you must do to not only survive, but thrive.

Have you ever been driving and couldn't figure out how you got to your destination? I know I have. Your mind goes on autopilot and you make all the right turns to get to the location you visit often. This cannot only happen when you are driving but also in your life and business. You begin to operate on autopilot and as long as no one complains about your performance and you do not hit any major bumps in the road you just keep moving the same way you have been. This is your comfort zone. There are three types of comfort zones. You can find comfort in consistent success and not push yourself further. You can get stuck in a series of failures and decide not to try any more. You can get stuck because you are a perfectionist and keep waiting for things to be "perfect" before you make a move.

Regardless of the reason behind the comfort zone, it is a dangerous place to find yourself or your team. Let go of the excuse and "Do NOT Settle"!! If you settle in your comfort zone, you will never fulfill your full potential. You will never accomplish your vision. You will never truly live until you get outside of your comfort zone. Continue to push yourself and your team to accomplish even more. Continue to learn from any failures and to press toward the next goal. Continue to strive toward excellence, not perfection. Be prepared to make adjustments as you move along.

There have been many successful companies that have found themselves irrelevant because they got stuck in their comfort zone of success and allowed complacency to set it. When a leader stops innovating and looking for the next great thing in their industry, they can allow the next company to surpass them. Maintaining forward thinking in the planning process will help your company to continue to innovate. Your company must avoid complacency at all cost. Two great examples of this are Eastman Kodak and Research in Motion (RIM).

Eastman Kodak is a great example of a company that got complacent and stopped innovating. In 1976, they held 90% of the market share of photographic film sales in the United States. They coined the phrase in their advertising a "Kodak Moment". In the late 1990s, they failed to shift into digital technology development, even though they created the core technology. They stopped looking in the rearview mirror and stopped looking for new ideas to grow the company. As a result, they lost their market share and allowed other companies to take the lead in digital technology. They were too comfortable being on top and their leadership did not look forward effectively.

Another example is Research in Motion (RIM) and Blackberry. The company quickly moved to be the market leader in cellular technology, especially for businesses. Most companies in the 90s used the Blackberry as their go to phone for their employees. Despite this lead in the market, they were unable to maintain against companies like Apple and Android. The leadership did not pay attention to what was happening in the industry with Apple and Android technologies and almost as quickly as they rose to prominence they were no longer relevant. Complacency can take out any company regardless of industry or size.

Some complacency is connected to a fear of failing. When you get stuck on the question – 'What if I fail?', you cannot accomplish anything worthwhile. You have given up before you even start. I agree with Coach John Wooden when he said, "Failure isn't fatal, but failure to change might be." Your idea may fail, but you can learn from it and improve it the next time around. The true failure occurs when we stop making the change necessary for our lives, our careers and our businesses to keep growing and maintain their relevance. If you allow failure and/or comfort with the minimum success to keep you in one place too long, stagnation will set in and that is never a good thing.

Complacency unchecked is the comfort zone you and your team can fall in over time. To get and stay out, you must fully understand what these comfort zones look like.

There are three types of comfort zones:

Comfort Zone of Success - Once you find the success you seek, there is a risk that you will get comfortable and complacent. Remember success is a journey not a destination. The mark of success continues to move as you accomplish each goal. In success, you can begin to work on autopilot. Success continues to come but you never achieve more than you did the last time. You have officially entered the comfort zone. You are not pushing yourself anymore. You are just happy with the status quo. No one is pushing you anymore because you are still ahead or at par with your peers. Your superiors do not want to upset you by asking for more. They are content with your consistent level of success.

Comfort Zone of Failure - In contrast, there is the comfort zone of failure. You can get comfortable after you've had a series of failures. You just decide not to take any risks. You stay in that safe box where you can easily find your success again. It doesn't challenge you. It's just comfortable. Leaders must be willing to take risks. Use your fear as a motivator. I now decide to pursue the goals that I'm afraid of instead of the ones that seem easy. I now look for the opportunity in the fear.

Comfort Zone of Perfection - The comfort zone of perfection is a space where you are so busy trying to make things perfect before you release them that you never get anything done. Excellence should be the goal not perfection. Perfection is an ideal and not a reality. A desire for perfection will not get you to your goals. You never know what you have until you release it. While you are trying to make it perfect, your competition is releasing it and then fixing any issues as they arise. The important thing is that they made a move and released their work in excellence.

Experiencing both success and failures, I understand being complacent and ending up in a comfort zone. On several occasions in my life, I have found myself in a comfort zone. I wish I could tell you differently, but I can't. It is easy to get stuck in there and not get out. The hard part is getting out. You have to make a conscious effort to keep from getting stuck there. I have learned over the years to be intentional and you will get out of it quickly.

At one point, I found myself stuck after having a serious of failures – job layoff, failed marriage, divorce, and debt. I was content just getting by. Small success was better than none at all. I felt as long as I played it safe, then I wouldn't have to worry about failing again. Well, I was wrong. I still had things happening. I still had struggles. At one point, I couldn't even get an interview for a job. Jobs I knew I was overqualified for, but I just wanted at job and to run my business on the side during this period.

Thankfully, as I mentioned in the preface, my good friend, Shelby pressed the right button and I began to move outside my comfort zone. While I was proud of the work I was doing with my business, I knew she was right. I didn't want to hear it or receive it at first. Her words haunted me for months.

I took a journey to rediscover who I am and what I should be doing. So when my friend at lunch asked me about my rates for consulting, it clicked. It all worked together to get me here to help you get out and stay out of your comfort zone. Success doesn't exist in complacency.

Regardless of the reasons that cause you and your team to get stuck in a space where you are settling for the minimum success, you must shake things up and reach for a more aggressive goal. You do not have to be defined by your last failure or success for that matter. Do not be afraid to keep raising the bar for yourself and your team. There is only stagnation in the comfort zone. Keep moving like a river. Each success should lead to the next one.

To make sure your team is doing what it takes to not become complacent, create a process to encourage new ideas and a desire to continue raising the bar. As a leader, you must know your competition and your industry. Remember that there are always new challenges and opportunities that you need to consider pursuing. Establish a process for deciding which opportunities you will pursue. You can maintain your success with consistent focus and stay aware of your business environment.

ACTION STEPS

1. Do identify whether your team is complacent.

Look at what's happening with your team. Are you seeing the signs of complacency? If so, don't ignore the signs. Talk with your team. Get their feedback. Admit that complacency exists so you can begin to move out of it.

2. Make the decision to get out of complacency.

Now that you know complacency exists, you must decide that today you're going to do something different to move out of it. It can be a small change at first. Look at the causes of complacency and begin to implement the fix.

3. Work with your team daily on staying out of complacency.

Each day, decide on one thing you can do different to make the shift out of complacency. Daily focus is what you and your team will need to get back to growth and progress. Set some goals. Write them down. Post them everywhere. Motivate each other daily. Learn from any setbacks and keep it moving. Don't slow down no matter what obstacles you face.

Application of "Do NOT Settle"

Getting out of complacency has often been critical to many of my clients. Often, we cannot find the success we seek professionally because we're stuck personally. I have helped clients pressed past all the excuses they have believed for years so they can walk fully in their greatness. There is greatness in all of us. There is greatness in every person on your team. As the leader, you just need to tap into it and pull it out of them.

One of my clients is now experiencing a rebirth of sorts. She spent her professional career as a CPA and now is pursuing her artistic endeavors as a visual artist. Drawing and painting were always important to her, but years of corporate work and raising a family began to take precedent. She looked up almost 20 years later and she was stuck in the "my family comes first" zone of complacency. Of course, her family was important, but she needed to be fulfilled to be the best wife and mother.

Now that she is drawing and painting again, she is happier and more fulfilled. Her family now has a woman who has so much more to give. She finds pleasure in creating and is energized to do so much more at home, at work and in the community. It's beautiful to see a person get outside their comfort zone and experience the fullness that exists there.

REMEMBER THE BENEFITS

- You will move yourself out of your comfort zone and avoid complacency.
- You will continue to press past your last success and seek the next goal.
- You will learn from failure and not let it slow you down.
- You will increase productivity consistently and your team will be motivated to keep taking it to the next level.

Assess Your Team

Do you currently see signs that your team is complacent?

_____

_____

_____

_____

What is your current way of addressing complacency?

_____

_____

_____

_____

Based on what you've read so far, what changes do you feel you need to make?

_____

_____

_____

_____

REFERENCES

1. Excuses: Their effective role in the negotiation of reality., Snyder, C. R.; Higgins, Raymond L.; Psychological Bulletin, Vol 104(1), Jul 1988, 23-35.
2. Letting Sleeping Truths Lie, Marvin Henberg, Canadian Journal of Philosophy, Vol. 16, No. 2 (Jun., 1986), pp. 281-295
3. Fraudulent Excuse Making Among College Students, Article in Teaching of Psychology 19(2):90-93 • April 1992. The Goals of Excuses and Communication Strategies Related to Causal Perceptions; Bernard Weiner, Alice Figueroa-Munioz, Craig Kakihara, ..., Feb 1, 1991
4. Age and excuses for forgetting: self-handicapping versus damage-control strategies. Erber JT1, Prager IG. International Journal on Aging and Human Development. 2000;50(3):201-14.
5. Study demonstrates that writing goals enhances goal achievement — Dominican University of California. Matthews, Gail. May 2015, Ninth Annual International Conference of the Psychology Research Unit of Athens Institute for Education and Research (ATINER).
6. Handicapping: the effects of its source and frequency. McElroy JC1, Crant JM. J Appl Psychol. 2008 Jul;93(4):893-900.
7. Nearly 29% of Employees Considered Unproductive, Survey Found. Proudfood Consulting. Insurance Journal. July 2016

8. The New Science of Building Great Teams. Pentland, Alex. Harvard Business Review. APRIL 2012.
9. The Five Dysfunctions of a Team. Lencioni, Patrick. 2012
10. Employee Engagement & the American Workplace. Valentino, Katie. Perspectives. February 2017
11. Study demonstrates that writing goals enhances goal achievement — Dominican University of California. Matthews, Gail. May 2015, Ninth Annual International Conference of the Psychology Research Unit of Athens Institute for Education and Research (ATINER).
12. Experimental Tests of the Endowment Effect and the Coase Theorem. Daniel Kahneman, Jack L. Knetsch and Richard H. Thaler. Journal of Political Economy, Vol. 98, No. 6 (Dec., 1990), pp. 1325-1348
13. Why Aren't You Delegating? Gallo, Amy. Harvard Business Review. JULY 26, 2012
14. Institute for Corporate Productivity Time Management Study. June 2007
15. Research: Delegating More Can Increase Your Earnings. Hubbard, Thomas N. Harvard Business Review . AUGUST 12, 2016
16. Delegating: A Huge Management Challenge for Entrepreneurs. Sangeeta Bharadwaj Badal and Bryant Ott. Gallop Business Journal. April 2015

Tracie L. James

Excuse Proof Leadership

ABOUT THE AUTHOR

Tracie L. James is a Leadership Strategist, Speaker and Author based in Houston, TX. Tracie has 20 plus years of experience in various aspects of business professionalism. She has extensive experience in sales and marketing that covers retail, account management, leadership development, business start-up, market strategy, program management, marketing, event planning, workshop facilitation and training. Tracie is a political strategist who has successfully managed a campaign for local city council and is called to provide strategic and tactical support to several candidates running for local and state offices. Tracie has worked with individuals, organizations and entities that are in the non-profit, municipal government, community, consumer goods, retail sales, and creative arts areas. She is passionate about nurturing individuals and collectives step beyond their proven potential and rethink possibilities of success.

WHO WANTS TO GET PAST THE EXCUSES & BECOME AN EXCUSE PROOF LEADER?!

Tracie James' straight forward yet fun style teaches leaders how to improve their problem solving skills so they will move their team toward more consistent success.

HOW TO USE TRACIE L. JAMES

1. KEYNOTE ADDRESS
2. LEADERSHIP DEVELOPMENT
3. LEADERSHIP STRATEGY

"Very informative message, (Tracie) gave great innovative ideas." Mary F.

FROM THE MEDIA TO YOUR STAGE

Tracie has been featured on NBC, ABC, and CBS, as well as in newspapers and magazines. Tracie's entertaining style is full of wisdom that will help your leaders achieve better results consistently.

"Great. Well worth the time and money..." Frank N.

When she presents, Tracie delivers her message with Southern charm infused with wisdom from her 20 years of business experience. She connects with the audience and delivers the "IT" factor that the audience will remember.

DATES ARE LIMITED.

REQUEST TRACIE L. JAMES FOR YOUR NEXT EVENT TODAY!

WWW.TRACIELJAMES.COM

www.ingramcontent.com/pod-product-compliance
Lightning Source LLC
Chambersburg PA
CBHW071604200326
41519CB00021BB/6857